Dog Collar

Inspiring stories of clergy and their dogs

RICHARD SURMAN

Collins

Collins

a division of HarperCollins Publishers

77-85 Fulham Palace Road, London W6 8JB

www.collins.co.uk

First published in Great Britain in 2007 by HarperCollins Publishers

1

A catalogue record for this book is available from the British Library.

isbn-13 978-0-00-724164-4

Design by Susie Bell

Printed and bound in Hong Kong by Printing Express

Contents

Introduction

Having worked on several books featuring the clergy of Britain and their cats, I couldn't help but notice that many of the people I contacted during the course of my research were dog owners, some rather indignant that I should be asking as to whether or not they had cats. It occurred to me that it would be great fun to pay tribute to the dog-loving members of the English clergy, as a contrast to tracking down and photographing sometimes decidedly truculent cats.

Dogs are as a rule so much more biddable, and the nature of the relationship between dog and owner is quite

different to that of a cat and its so-called 'owner'. Hence the idea of producing a book that featured dogs and their owners jointly. The dog collar naturally suggested itself as central punning concept to pull the whole thing together, and so I set out to explore the fellowship between dog and human, a worthy intention that became subverted by the subjects! Certainly there was much to discover about the nature of the relationships between the dogs and their owners, but so many of the dogs I met were such characters: 'barking' mad, eccentric, funny, obsessive, and it's very hard to remain serious when confronted with dogs that have such an exuberant love of life. The clergy I met were great characters too, also funny, perhaps a bit eccentric, and it was they who perceived the gentle humour of the whole project. As a result the book has taken on a lighter tone than perhaps originally envisaged, although affection between dog and owner remains a constant and touching element throughout.

A grateful parishioner wrote to one of the clergy featured in this book as follows, demonstrating the affection dogs can inspire:

'On behalf of all the family, we would like to thank you for conducting such a lovely service for Dad yesterday. It was very uplifting, just as Dad would have wished, and your tribute to him was nicely put, and of course we had the added bonus of Jack's presence. We could imagine Dad smiling as we approached the little church: he loved to see you and Jack waiting to welcome him at the entrance gate. So special thanks to Jack. His presence was what Dad would have called the icing on the cake, and we would agree.'

In case you are wondering what a cat person is doing producing a book about dogs, I am a sometime dog person too. We had gentle Max, a Golden Retriever who withstood my children's attempts to ride him with cheerful fortitude. I also remember with great affection Barney, our childhood Red Setter (and equally vividly, but with less affection, a psychotic and unfortunate Bull terrier called Rasher).

I am very grateful to everyone who took part: the whole venture was highly enjoyable, and I only got nipped once (you know who you are!) And special thanks to my publisher, Ian Metcalfe, who agreed so readily to take the book on.

For Blanca, Carlos and Gabriel

The Rev. Marilyn Adsetts, Cherry and Daisy

St David's Church, Rhymney

'Cherry and Daisy make me laugh'

In Marilyn Adsett's previous parish, in Ipswich, pastoral visiting used to be a particular pleasure, since her Labradors Cherry and Beatrice would accompany her, and all three shared a love of walking on the coastal sand dunes. Marilyn recalls how she could hardly see the dogs, as their colour was a perfect camouflage against the sand.

Marilyn is now Vicar of Rhymney and Abertysswg, a Church of Wales parish in the Welsh Valleys, a decidedly less coastal but still geographically distinctive location. As Beatrice got older, Marilyn decided to acquire another Labrador, this time a lighter coloured, show-bred dog from a farm in Ludlow. Both Cherry and Beatrice were aghast at this new arrival; Beatrice retreated under a table to avoid the boisterous puppy, and Cherry simply ignored her. In time Daisy (as the new arrival was called) got the message, and tempered her youthful boisterousness – slightly. Meanwhile Beatrice moved away, leaving Cherry bereft – until she realised that she had the makings of a new companion in Daisy. In due course these two have become firm friends, although Cherry remains somewhat confused by Daisy's inexhaustible energy, while Daisy finds it difficult to understand why Cherry doesn't want to keep on running forever.

One problem that has arisen is that Cherry won't go on parish visits without a canine companion; but to take Daisy would, in Marilyn's words, 'be tantamount to pastoral demolition', so at present Cherry finds herself, too, left behind. Marilyn has tried using the internet as a resource for dog-training. I'm not sure quite how that works; maybe via a serious of admonishing e-mails. A hefty dose of dog school is also helping to calm Daisy down – it seems there is an agency in the Rhymney area that offers dog training on the one hand, and 'door supervisor' (corporate speak for 'bouncer') training on the other. So perhaps we'll see Daisy flexing her muscles outside the local nightclub at some point in the future.

Nonetheless, while the dogs don't have access to the open beaches of East Anglia, they do have the mountains and hills of Wales on which to walk, which they do regularly in company with Marilyn, so Cherry doesn't miss out on walks entirely, and Daisy gets a chance to run off some of her excess energy – the only hazard is dodging the occasional out of control mountain-biker!

The Rev. John Angle and Poppy

Church of St. Michael the Archangel, North Cadbury

'Dogs are fun: Poppy helps me relax, slows me down and gives me a sense of well being'

Under normal circumstances, Poppy is a well-behaved young dog, but this irrepressible young Scottish Labrador is football-mad: show her a football, and she transforms into a leaping, ball-grabbing canine soccer star. Her ability to head the ball is uncanny, and if there were a world cup for dog soccer, Poppy would surely be on the national team as a striker! John Angle may say she slows him down, but I think that in Poppy's case, that would have to depend very much on the definition of the phrase. If by 'slowing down', one means that one literally goes slower then, no: the only kind of relaxation that Poppy offers is that of becoming part of her joyful world. You could not possibly be out with Poppy and her football, and spare even a second to think about the travails of the outside world. You'd be too busy throwing headers, watching her dribble the ball through the shrubs and saying 'That's enough, Poppy.' It's a different kind of relaxation, though highly effective.

Poppy is the Angles' second Labrador: the first, Rosie, was a true pastoral assistant, who loved young people, figuring significantly in John Angle's work with them. He had been a deputy headmaster in Bristol before turning to the ministry, and his subsequent work has involved him and his wife Janet in, among other things, fostering.

However troubled the child, having Rosie around was a four-legged blessing. She could sense when someone was worried, and was always on hand to offer consolation.

Poppy is not yet a Rosie in that way, but all dogs have their own distinct character, and Poppy is shining in other ways. Apart from her astonishing skills with a ball, she travels around in John's car, keeping him company as he works his way around his nine North Cadbury parishes; she also puts in star appearances at the local primary school (footballs are hastily put away before she arrives). Poppy is a dog who does a lot of liking of other people and animals. She likes children, older folk, livestock, other dogs, cats – and so on. She does a lot of liking with the Angles' Abyssinian cat, Abi, too. It's taken about fifteen months for Abi to appreciate this intrusive interest in her wellbeing, but now she picks her routes around the house in spaces that Poppy can't quite reach. Not that Poppy even notices: the world she inhabits is a world where everyone and everything get on, a world of play and of assured affection.

The Rev. Alan Beardsmore and Nelson, a.k.a. Nellie

Church of St Andrew, Eaton

'Nellie helps me to keep a sense of perspective on life – she's a great and loving companion'

If there was a competition for the dog with the most soulful, heart-melting expression, then surely Nellie would win it hands down. This gravely beautiful and thoroughly gentle English Setter belongs to the Rev. Alan Beardsmore, an ex-naval chaplain who is now Vicar of St Andrew's, Eaton. Although he grew up in the company of Irish Setters, running wild in Richmond Park, Alan's first dog of his own, Bernard, was a West Highland Terrier. But his second dog, Boots, came from the English Setter Rescue Society, and was joined by another English Setter – Toby – from the same source. The two dogs became great companions; setters always do tend to do better in pairs. The only difference between them was that Boots was racy, while Toby was slow. So they'd walk on a link chain, with Boots acting as Toby's 'tug'.

This link chain led to an amusing consequence. One day the two dogs had been left together in the vicarage garden, linked by their chain, with the local hunt assembling for a meet close by. Boots and Toby, inspired perhaps by the excitement of the hounds, decided to follow, leaped the garden fence and set off in pursuit of the hounds. By the time they caught up a fox had been sighted, and the hunt was in full cry. Up dashed Boots and Toby, enthusiastically joining in, while their link chain acted as a sort of sweep, sending the hounds tumbling and rolling willy-nilly. No attempts by the master of hounds could discourage them, and the day's hunt fell apart in a shambles of spread-eagled beagles and milling horses. The master of the hunt, out of deference to Alan's position as local vicar, refrained from expressing his feelings too vividly, but Allan was left in no doubt that Boots and Toby were far from the hunt's favourite dogs.

After a period of being without a dog, Alan's children suggested that it was time for him to have another English Setter. They went to a local breeder with the intention of getting an Orange Belton dog to be named 'Nelson', but came away from the breeder with a Blue Belton bitch. So 'Nelson' became 'Nellie'. They are inseparable: Nellie is a big softy, who likes nothing better than to clamber onto Alan's lap. She accompanies him even to morning and evening prayers. Nellie's face looks as if she's carrying the cares of the world on her shoulders but when one looks at how she sits, close and content with Alan, her inner contentment is clear.

The Rev. John Beauchamp, Trevor and Alfie

**Church of St Michael the Archangel,
and St Luke's Church, Beccles**

'Dog is not by accident God spelt backwards'

Trevor and Alfie are different from all the other dogs featured in this book, as their principal role is as guide dogs to John Beauchamp, the blind Vicar of Beccles. John Beauchamp's first guide dog was Farina, who accompanied him through his theology studies at Wycliffe Hall, where she slept patiently through all the lectures, only occasionally interrupting with a genteel snore. Farina guided John for many years, and only retired very reluctantly. 'It's a difficult

and demanding job, and one which cannot supply the kind of routine that most dogs enjoy', John points out.

But the breed, a first cross between Golden Retriever and Labrador, is clearly up to the job. Farina's place was taken by Trevor who, at the age of ten and a half, simply decided one day to retire: he just sat down, as if to say 'That's enough; now it's someone else's turn'. But he did not need to be pensioned off: he simply became a pet dog for Natalie Beauchamp, John's wife. This left an opening for the position as guide for John, which was filled by Alfie.

Alfie, like all dogs in guiding work, has an uncanny sense of when it is time to play, and when it is time to work, and, according to John, is shaping up very well. It is inspiring to come across a dog that can be totally daft and soppy at one moment, and in an instant snap to full attention, knowing that there is work to be done. John particularly values the help his two dogs do, in relation to comforting the bereaved, and as a point of interest with his parishioners, all of whom love both Alfie and Trevor. The only bone of contention is when John plays the flute, which, as a former music teacher, he does very well. Trevor was content enough to sit through John's flute playing with a resigned, slightly pained look on his face; Alfie only has to see John pick up the flute, to make a run for the furthest corner of the house, where he lies, paws over his ears, until the music dies down.

Since the Beauchamps' children have left home, both Trevor and Alfie have become an even more important part of the family. John commented that although they are both guide dogs, they are very relaxing to have around, and give great pleasure by virtue of their domestic company – and are clearly regarded with much affection in regard to their 'dogginess', as well as being respected for their work.

The Very Rev. David Brindley and Charlie

Portsmouth Cathedral

'I don't quite know why I got Charlie, but I'm very glad I did'

One only has to see David Brindley out with Charlie, an English Springer Spaniel, to realise that here is a really affectionate partnership. David doesn't really have an explanation for why he got Charlie, who came from a farm in Abingdon. 'Perhaps it was partly to encourage myself to exercise,' he says. And exercise there certainly was, in abundance, including sponsored walks, notably one along the length of the Warwick Way, during which £6000 was raised, mostly from pubs along the way, for the local hospice. But whatever motivated him to get Charlie, back when he was Rector of St Mary's, Warwick, it's been a most successful partnership.

Charlie took a lead rôle in two pet services at St Mary's – that is to say, his lead was firmly attached to a chair, as he seemed more interested in playing with the assorted dogs, cats, gerbils, stick insects and snakes in attendance (although perhaps the idea of 'playing' with snakes and stick insects is a bit fanciful – but they can be barked at). Now David is Dean of Portsmouth Cathedral, and he and Charlie still take long walks in the New Forest and on the South Downs, of eight to ten miles and with a pub lunch in the middle. I wonder which is the stronger motivating force

– whether it is Charlie's love of walks that helps the Dean to walk off the pub lunches, or whether the long walks with Charlie provide a perfect excuse for a pub lunch!

Portsmouth Cathedral is probably the most 'animal friendly' of the places that appears in Dog Collar. Ivor the cathedral cat featured in a previous book, and has to be mentioned here, as he figures, rather mischievously, in

Charlie's life. Charlie often goes over to the cathedral with David, and the cathedral is traditionally Ivor's territory. There are no confrontations as such, but once Ivor knows that Charlie's lead is firmly attached to a chair leg outside one of the offices that lead off the cloister passageway, he slowly strolls into sight at the end of the passage, and sits down, washing painstakingly until Charlie sees him. Charlie hurls himself towards Ivor, only to be held back by his lead: Charlie starts to bark; Ivor walks slowly out of view. He waits round the corner until Charlie has settled down again, and then slowly reverses his route, walking slowly until he comes into Charlie's line of sight. Ivor then sits innocently until a response is again elicited, and then, before anyone can come out to reproach him, walks slowly out of sight again. I fear that one day Charlie's charge will overcome the weight of the chair holding him and he will hurtle down the passageway in pursuit of Ivor, with the chair in tow. Even the easy informality of Portsmouth Cathedral might be shaken by the sight and sound of Ivor dashing across the nave with Charlie and chair in hot pursuit.

Charlie has his own rounds: he always gets a cheery greeting from everyone in the cathedral, and the seafront dog-walking fraternity are a daily fixture. David and Charlie always take in a bracing coastal walk before matins, during which Charlie meets his pal Toffee, the dog of the local Unitarian minister. Even in a Force Seven wind, the dogs romp around on top of the fortified sea walls. A happy dog, a contented man: a perfect partnership.

The Rev. Stephen Buckley and Maisie

All Saints' Church, Sedgley

'I get uncomplicated love, friendship and affection from Maisie, although I suspect that it's all based on food!'

The Rev. Stephen Buckley and his wife Christine had always been of a feline persuasion, until three years ago, when a friend offered them a foundling Bearded Collie cross. 'She's just right for you,' enthused their friend, 'She matches your beard and hair, Stephen'. Whether or not Maisie really matched Stephen Buckley's fine head of hair and splendid beard, she was just right for the Buckleys, who now describe themselves as staunchly 'doggist'.

Stephen is now Team Rector of All Saints, Sedgley, together with St Andrew the Straits and St Peter's, Upper Gornal, but came to the ministry from a theatrical background. In addition to his general parish work, he is also involved in community justice schemes, most notably a restorative justice programme run by the Dudley Youth Offending Scheme. Maisie's involvement with parish life goes as far as attending morning prayers with Stephen, and the Friday morning service, where she meets her fan club, a small group of kindly old ladies. Stephen is Chaplain to the local ATC (Air Training Corps) squadron, and at one point he considered offering Maisie's services as mascot, but decided that she was a bit too unreliable. I wouldn't go that far: Maisie is jolly, ebullient and a bit soppy, a dog who rolls on the carpet flapping her paws in the air to get one to tickle her under the arms – which attention she accompanies with groans of ecstasy – but smart enough to pull every trick in the book to entice those ever-present dog treats out of Stephen's pocket, and into her mouth. One of Maisie's great contributions to family welfare is in helping Christine, who suffers from the 'winter blues'. Maisie's insistence on being taken out for walks, even in the most miserable weather, means that Christine is assured of her daily dose of outdoor light!

Maisie found it difficult to settle in at first, but, after a couple of disappearing episodes, came to relish life at the vicarage. She's a mixture of the bold and the craven: Maisie loves meeting other dogs on their local walks through nearby fields and parks – as long as they aren't too large. She is always inviting other (small) dogs to chase her, while trying to avoid being chased – or even seen – by larger dogs. This intermittent bravado crumbles entirely in the face of a visit to the vets, when Maisie will cry, whine and howl as though she is being questioned by the inquisition. Oh yes, and she can't stand cats.

The Rev. Dr Andrew Bunch and Thea

St Giles' Church, Oxford

'A home is empty without a dog'

A caller to the Rev. Andrew Bunch's North Oxford vicarage may well find that the door is answered by Thea, a tall soulful Red Setter. The visitor will then be subject to scrutiny by Thea, who may decide to take the visitor's wrist gently in her mouth, as if to say, 'Just relax. Your pulse is way too high. We can sort everything out here. By the way, did I tell you that you're my favourite person?' This is solid understated affection. No big noise or fuss, just physical contact and solicitous canine therapy. The caller will then be guided by Thea (clutching the visitor's wrist firmly, but gently, in a soft wet mouth) into Andrew's study.

Before becoming a vicar, Andrew Bunch was a marine seismologist. When it is suggested that it's an unusual career change he demurs: 'It's not so much of a change. Both occupations are concerned with powers that shake the world.' His first canine companion was Zara, the first of four Red Setters; she used to accompany him to his research laboratories. A second red setter – Clare – replaced Zara, and was with the Bunches while Andrew worked as a team vicar in Windsor. Clare was 'a bit short on brain', although it was with Clare that Andrew and his wife Kathryn found out just how good Red Setters are with children. Clare was joined by Lucy, who was plagued with ill health, dying at four and a half, leaving Clare bereft.

Then, finally, came Thea. She's a bright, agile and affectionate dog, who manages her relationships in the family and her physical surroundings with equal aplomb. Kathryn is the food provider, Andrew is for company, as he's more often in the house; and when both Kathryn and Andrew are in at the same time, Thea divides her attention equally between them. Closed doors can be hooked open with a paw, settees can be sneaked onto quietly, and there is always the doorbell to answer.

Thea has to be watched when out for a walk, as she has a phenomenal turn of speed, and cannot resist greeting other dogs. Andrew, being a dog-lover, often makes a fuss of dogs that they meet during their walks. Thea shows no resentment: she in her turn makes a fuss of the other dog's owner, and has charmed more than her fair share of dog biscuits from these chance encounters. Then there is Thea's extraordinary attention to visitors. I haven't come across a dog who makes one feel quite so welcome, so 'at home'. No wonder Andrew Bunch describes her as a 'wonderful ice-breaker'.

The Rev. Celia Carter and Mahdi

Holy Cross Church, Avening

*'My dogs are a source of love and affection...
animals have incredible sensitivity'*

The Rev. Celia Carter is Priest in Charge of Avening and Cherington parishes, two sleepy and traditional English villages on the western slopes of the Cotswolds. By coincidence her family home is in Avening too, a rambling Georgian house and farm, reminiscent of Trollope's Barsetshire Chronicles.

Celia Carter grew up on Dartmoor, surrounded by a melange of dogs, and dogs have recurred as a feature in highly unusual circumstances throughout Celia's life. As a young wife, she joined her husband, the late Colonel Stewart Carter OBE, in Oman, where he was commanding the Trucial Oman Scouts. It was highly unusual for a European woman to be in Arabia at that time, and the only way that Celia could travel in the desert with her husband was to dress as a young soldier. As it was considered unacceptable to have a dog as a pet, Col. Carter had asked Celia to discreetly bring out a Norfolk Terrier puppy (which looked a bit like a cross between a squirrel and a rabbit) and Celia and her dog travelled in 'masquerade', Celia as a trooper, and by tacit agreement with the Bedouin who accompanied them, the dog was deemed a 'squirrel'. I wonder how the barking was explained?

Celia's present canine companion is another Norfolk Terrier, Mahdi (Arabic for 'soft'), as was her predecessor Tara. When Tara wasn't keeping Celia company, she spent much of her time helping to keep sheep out of the garden, and one of her favourite duties was to marshal the menagerie that takes part in Christmas Eve services. This includes Shetland ponies who double as both donkeys and reindeer, sheep, lambs, piglets and chickens, whose delight at finding themselves in the fresh straw of the manger induces a frenzy of egg laying.

Mahdi is only a puppy at present, so small she'll fit into a coat pocket. But already she's showing signs of the dash and vigour that characterises the breed. Putting her down on the ground is like setting down a wind-up toy. Before her feet have reached the ground, Mahdi's legs are making a frantic running motion, and as soon as they're in contact with the ground, whoosh – off she goes. She has been introduced to the parish, and her ears are already a familiar sight in the area, poking up inquisitively above Celia's car window sill. It must be an odd view of the world for Mahdi, as yet so small that all she can see from the car's seat are tree-tops and sky.

The Rev. Margot Davies and Demi

Church of St John-in-the-fields, Halsetown

'In ministry there are things that you cannot share – dogs alleviate the pressure that brings'

Demi is a friendly, curious and extremely bouncy multi-component cross-breed, with an engagingly soppy grin. Margot Davies describes her as a 'collie-badger cross'. There's certainly Border Collie in there somewhere, as evidenced by Demi's love of bouncing through the grass, and the characteristic crouching stance of a sheepdog about to go to work. As to the rest, one can only imagine! She came from a local animal rescue centre, where she'd been picked up as a stray. The centre was initially reluctant for Demi to come to the vicarage, as there was no clearly defined enclosed space for her. However, the impression made by Demi on the family when they visited her at the rescue centre must have been reciprocated, for shortly afterwards, Margot received a call saying that Demi had been so depressed since their first visit, they'd better come and get her as soon as possible – enclosed yard or not.

From the instant that she left the centre, Demi became entirely their dog. They didn't have to house-train her: she neither attempted to go where she was not permitted, such as upstairs, nor to cadge food. Demi just wants to be with the family. She'll round them up like a small flock of errant sheep, trying to move everyone in the direction of the sitting room. Visitors are normally greeted with enthusiasm; she seized the end of my pencil while I was taking notes, as if she had something particular to say – perhaps along the lines of 'Write how much I like them; and maybe an extra meal each day might be a good idea?'

Demi has a curious way of watching approaching visitors: there's a redundant cat flap set into the side door, and at the sound of footsteps, the flap will quietly open outwards, until Demi's white nose pokes through. If she likes the look of the visitor, then fine. If not, she scoots round to the front door in double quick time, and lets rip a fusillade of warning barks. Her day is often spent in Margot Davies's study – either wound around Margot's chair, or more often than not, trying to clamber up onto her lap.

Demi is a dog whose time is divided neatly between the search for comfort and delight in exuberant exercise. She bounds through the long grass with Margot, or goes with Margot's artist husband David on long cliff-top walks.

The Rev. Karen Elsworth and Pippa

Church of St Peter and St Paul, Yalding with St Margaret's, Collier Street

'She's a wonderful timewaster, who takes me away from the more sombre aspects of life'

Karen Elsworth was ordained last September at Rochester, and is curate of St Peter and St Paul, Yalding and St Margaret's, Collier Street. She is also a chartered physiotherapist, who came to live in England with her family nineteen years ago, from Zimbabwe; and she still practices physiotherapy part time. The family had kept dogs in Africa, a Border Collie and two other dogs whose genetic antecedents were 'unknowable'. Having had a border collie in Africa, the family decided to get another, and son Damon chose Pippa from a farm litter.

Pippa suffered an early setback, losing a hind leg in a road accident at three months. But being young, she didn't let that impede her in any way, and many visitors simply don't realise at first that Pippa is a three-legged dog: she runs regular 14-milers with Karen's husband Sandy, an amateur long distance runner. She's an avid basketball player, as attested by the many deflated basket balls that litter their garden: when Damon comes home from university, Pippa grabs a ball, and waits impatiently under the basket. When the game starts, Pippa's great leaps into the air, and high speed pursuit of the ball, gainsay her 'disability'.

Even more extraordinarily, Pippa also works, joining her sister at a nearby farm each week, where the two dogs happily herd turkeys and sheep. To compensate for the missing left rear leg, Pippa always goes right, while her sister Meg works to the left. Pippa practises her herding techniques at home too, mostly on Bandit, the long-suffering family cat. Bandit's only escape is that she, unlike Pippa, is allowed upstairs.

At home Pippa always greets everyone in the morning as if they are long lost friends returning from the wilderness. She is a great pastoral example of how to overcome adversity too, although Karen has a simpler reason for appreciating Pippa: 'She's just great fun to have around!'

The Rev. Tim Heaney and Holly

St James the Great, Dursley

'Holly gets me out on great country walks, and helps me feel connected to nature'

The Internet can be a great research tool - when Diane, the wife of the Rev. Tim Heaney, looked at the profile of different dog breeds to find one with a suitable profile for the family, she found that a Schnauzer would suit them best. They went to a Welsh breeder, but returned with Holly, an Airedale Terrier, and the mistake was only discovered when the Heaneys got home, by which time Holly had already worked her way into their hearts.

Tim and Diane's children had been asking for a dog for years, and Tim had always resisted on the grounds that they moved so frequently. But his appointment as Curate of Dursley in Gloucestershire, and the subsequent move to a house on the edge of glorious countryside, made all his objections redundant. Diane thought that it would be useful to have a dog on security grounds, and with his three daughters Rebekah, Samantha and Katharine also ranged against him, Tim's resolve collapsed.

And perhaps to his surprise, he thoroughly enjoys having Holly around. Holly is an irrepressible character, whose desire to play is insatiable, as is her enthusiasm for people. On the security front, Holly would simply exhaust any would-be miscreant. She bounces and bounds through life. Dursley's first glimpse of Holly was a press photo taken during the traditional beating of the bounds. Holly was caught mid air, leaping towards the photographer in enthusiastic greeting. She also caused quite a stir at the local primary school when she was introduced for the first time, appearing out of a blanket-covered box (although how Holly kept quiet and still in the box to achieve the desired surprise effect is something of a puzzle).

Tim wryly observes how curious it is that Holly came at the behest of the family females, yet he is always the one to walk her! In truth he and Holly have become close companions: they have some wonderful woodland walks on the other side of the valley, and she is a regular conversation starter around town. Holly even goes with Tim to the Parish Church of St James, where she has a particular pew reserved for her during morning prayers.

The only member of the family to be displaced by Holly's arrival was Gizzie the cat. When Holly arrived, he moved upstairs, and Holly was kept downstairs. Sadly, this didn't suit Gizzie, who simply packed her bags one day, and set off to find a dog-free home.

The Rev. Canon Francis Hewitt and Hamish

Church of St Peter and St Paul, Pickering

'A dog is a perfect companion, a combination of security, companionship and something to make a fuss over'

I first met Canon Hewitt some years ago, when I visited him to find out about his cat, Pushkin, for the book *Church Cats*. The Hewitts live in the North Yorkshire town of Pickering, where Francis Hewitt is Vicar of Pickering with Lockton and Levisham and was formerly Rural Dean. It's a peaceful place, on the edge of the North York Moors National Park, and attracts over twenty thousand visitors each year. I had no recollection of there being a dog in the household, and it was explained to me that on that previous visit, Hamish had been discreetly locked away upstairs in order to allow Pushkin, a friendly but frail old chap, an open field.

It now transpires that Francis and Brenda are principally a 'dog' family who had decided to have a cat. This goes all the way back to Francis Hewitt's time at theological college, when they rescued a puppy, keeping it concealed in a desk drawer until a cleaner heard it scrabbling around and ran for her life. He remembers how, 'the singing in chapel used to suddenly rise in volume to cover the puppy's whining.' The Hewitts have had deerhounds too in their time, and once when Francis Hewitt answered a call at the door in the small hours to find two pie-eyed youngsters, come to repent of their sins, they reconsidered on seeing and

hearing Barnabas (the deerhound), and decided to return at a more civilized time.

Meeting Hamish, a blissful tail-wagging machine masquerading as a Cocker Spaniel, I understood the Hewitts' canine enthusiasm: Hamish radiates pleasure at just about everything, almost losing his balance, as his stumpy tail fans the air like a broken propeller. He also sniffs a lot, like a perpetual vacuum machine. Francis Hewitt maintains that he could sniff for England (though I'd not heard that this was proposed for the next Dog Olympics). Of course, when he arrived as a puppy Hamish wasn't quite so enthusiastic about Pushkin – and the feeling was reciprocated. He soon learnt to sit very quietly whilst Pushkin delicately ate his food. And Pushkin also made it clear that any ball thrown was for his benefit, not Hamish's.

As the cat grew older, Hamish's light shone brighter, in particular where activities in the parish church were concerned. One of Hamish's more spectacular moments was during a confirmation service, at which he may have 'seen the light' or had some other epiphany, for without warning he leapt onto the archiepiscopal midriff, stumpy

tail going nineteen to the dozen. Hamish loves all things to do with parish life. At wedding interviews he is the first to leap up onto a chair, and he can't wait to attend wedding rehearsals (and Francis Hewitt has had to decline, on Hamish's behalf, an invitation to be a page boy). He always wags his way to Matins and to Evensong – which he sometimes accompanies with loud snores; and at home he 'helps' with the post. Home is where he assists Mrs Hewitt too, as she marks 'A' Level examination papers: Hamish's marking, however is more that of the 'toothmark' variety.

Hamish and the newspaper boy have developed an entertaining routine with which to wake up the household each morning. Hamish sits under the letter box, and the newspaper boy pushes the papers through, then pulls them back out again. This is repeated several times, with Hamish barking and leaping for the paper each time. But with other calls to make, the newspaper boy reluctantly has to let Hamish get the papers, upon which he gives them a good shake and a little chew before releasing them to their rightful owners, whose first task of the day is therefore to reassemble the patchwork of fragmented headlines.

The Rev. Anne Heywood and Coffee

St James's Church and St John's Church, Shaftesbury

'Coffee is my supportive companion, my right-hand man if you like, and very much a part of my ministry'

Coffee is a friendly and inquisitive mostly-Border-Collie, almost as much of a fixture in parish life as his owner, Anne Heywood, whom he accompanies and watches over attentively. Anne is Team Vicar in the Shaston Team Ministry, responsible for (among other things) the churches of two parishes, St James's and St John's. And parish life includes Coffee, who attends all the services, but whose favourite service is one at St John's, Enmore Green, where he meets a canine friend called Jack: the two dogs always sit together quietly until the 'peace', when both trot around exchanging salutations with various parishioners. Coffee is so popular among the parishioners that he gets regular wedding and baptism invitations, and has even had a buttonhole made up for him in the past. He attends school assemblies with Anne, and is the first to bark his appreciation if an achievement award is given.

The one area of domestic discord between Anne and Coffee is food. One can't help but admire his food plundering methodology: a veritable Viking raider of larders, pantries and tables, Coffee has been found under a table eating the Harvest loaves, hunks of Brie cheese, entire quiches; on one occasion he even wolfed down a half pound of butter and half a Wensleydale cheese.

But he does have a considerate side – Anne is always struck by how he seems to always know when someone is downhearted or troubled; he'll immediately go to them, not to fuss, but just to sit close, as if expressing that he knows what it is to be troubled. In turn, he has someone who sits close to him if he's feeling particularly under the weather – Samson the cat. And indeed Coffee does have his own troubles, having recently been diagnosed with lymphoma: he's now on a strictly controlled diet, which he doesn't find easy. Anne told me how one night he was so desperate for food that he appeared by her bedside one night with a can of cat food in his mouth.

Samson, like Coffee, is a rescue animal, a great bruiser of a black cat. People bring their dogs to meet Samson, in order for them to learn a bit of cat-respect! But with Coffee, Samson is as gentle as a lamb. He headbutts him affectionately as they pass, and when Coffee is resting – particularly after a session of medical treatment at the vets – Samson, who will have been waiting restlessly for Coffee to come home, will quietly lie beside him until he feels better.

Ill-health apart, Coffee is a great character. His CV includes personal appearances in at least fourteen nativity plays, and he made a semi-professional acting debut recently. Thankfully medical treatment and home care are proving highly effective. Just a few days ago he was sufficiently recovered to walk alongside the band in the Shaftesbury Town Carnival, and managed to pinch a bag of crisps from a spectator! Let's hope that he continues to respond to treatment, for he's a much-loved family dog – and an honorary parish member.

The Rev. Stephen Hollinghurst and Max

St Andrew's Church, Presteigne

'Max makes me laugh: I love his unquestioning loyalty and appreciation'

When Stephen Hollinghurst's first dog, a tricoloured Cocker Spaniel called Kipper, died, the thought of replacing him was almost too much. How does one replace such a well-loved companion? Especially one with party tricks such as lying under a beer keg and emptying the drip tray (earning him the 'Most Inebriated Dog of the Year Award'), shredding shoelaces, and eating whole tubs of garlic capsules. It would take a dog of great character to take Kipper's place.

And along came Max, a dog of completely different tastes – though perhaps equally populist. Max's preoccupations are different to those of Kipper. Whereas Kipper regularly attended parish social events (when he was sober enough), Max stays at home. Why? Because all Max wants to do is play ball. He is a Peter Pan sort of dog – a ten-year-old Springer Spaniel who thinks he's still a puppy. Any ball, any size, colour, deflated or inflated, hard or soft. He just can't get through the loveable delinquent stage. Trying to get a picture of Max by himself was an ordeal – for him. He'd obey Stephen's command to sit or lie, and hold the pose, quivering with frustration, for a few seconds – before exploding off after another ball. Max is eager to please; he just doesn't have time to hang around.

Inside the house Max has to contend with Stephen Hollinghurst's peculiarities. Not for nothing is Stephen described as the 'Rocking Rev' in the regional press. His study sports an impressive range of guitars, snappy hats, and showbiz ephemera; one of his regular fundraising gigs features a five piece choir called 'The OK Chorale', a combination of Wild West and high church at which the mind boggles. But vicars are allowed a sense of humour, and this is only one of Stephen's interests – I'm not going to go into his enthusiasm for steam trains and canals, except to note his suspicion that some Bishops, during ordination, secretly administer a large and addictive dose of transportation nostalgia.

The deal between dog and man is based around mutual tolerance of different interests: Max puts up with the singing and guitar playing, as long as Stephen plays with him regularly. And in general, it works. Who can remain frazzled after a tough PCC meeting when there's a crazy dog planting a ball at your feet, as if to say, 'Listen pal. Get a life. Throw a ball.'

The Rev. Pat Hopkins, and Millie, Ben, Misty and Harry

St Bartholomew's Church, Otford

'My dogs provide me with friendship and empathy'

The Rev. Pat Hopkins lives among a swirl of dogs, all of whom accompany her as she goes to St Bartholomew's, the parish church in the historic village of Otford in Kent.

These dogs are a curious selection. There's Millie, a red Norfolk Terrier, and the diminutive boss of all Pat's dogs. Then there's Ben, a brindle Cairn Terrier, who sometimes – against the odds in this household – likes to be alone. Misty is a black and tan Rottweiler, who came to enhance the security of the vicarage. She's a good guard dog, but is convinced that she is just another small dog when it comes to playing with the others. Last is Harry, a red miniature wire-haired Dachshund, who never stops playing.

Pat can often be seen walking over to the church with her dogs, a boisterous tangle of leads and excited canines, all of them delighted to be with Pat, and equally delighted to be going out together. Mille is the unquestioned leader of the pack, and when they all walk through nearby woodlands, Millie sets the tree-sniffing pattern, all the other dogs lining up to have a good smell after Millie has had her fill of whatever she has decided to sniff at. By the riverside too, Millie sets the pace. At the first sight of water, she leads a mad collective dash into the river. The ducks don't know what has hit them as this procession of dogs blunders blithely into the water. And when they meet them, Millie is a big hit with children.

At home, all the dogs have their own idiosyncrasies. Harry and Millie, pictured below, 'help' in the garden. The sight of a spade being wielded sends both into a frenzy: eagerly rooting up any new plantings, they then dash around trying to find a place where they, too, can dig a 'sympathetic' hole. Harry doesn't bother much with doors either. He's more likely to come flying into or out of the house through an open window. Ben joins in all this leaping and dashing: he is great friends with Harry, and the two of them chase each other in dizzying circles round the garden.

Although Millie is the boss, she puts up with Harry dragging her by her fur, which he does to get to the food first. The more curious deference is that of Misty, such a large and ferocious-looking dog, to Millie, a quarter of her size. Misty has also adopted Harry, who she seems to regard as her puppy, giving him a thorough daily wash and groom. Misty doesn't bother to bark at regular visitors; she leaves that to the smaller dogs, reserving her barking for any unexpected, and sometimes not-so-welcome callers.

The Rev. Alan Hughes and Harris

Church of the Holy Trinity, Berwick upon Tweed

'Harris is an example of unselfish love'

Septimus Spot, Shuma, Skye: the roll call of Jack Russells in the Rev. Alan Hughes's life goes on and on. Alan has had a passion for the breed right from the time, many years ago, when he first collected his wife-to-be, Susan, for a white tie ball. There was a Jack Russell sitting in the hall, who suddenly got up, walked over to Alan, sank its teeth into his shin, and then resumed its place as if nothing had happened.

One of Alan's early projects after ordination was to restore and revitalize a derelict church in Yorkshire, and during their time there, he and his wife found a Jack Russell breeder: they bought a puppy, naming him after the Scottish island of Skye. Skye accompanied them to a new project, the unification of four Yorkshire Dales parishes. This was a very busy family: not only did Alan have his church duties to attend to, but he was also serving as a battalion chaplain to the Parachute Regiment. He had trained as a free-fall parachutist when serving as a regular soldier in the Coldstream Guards in the 1960s – a useful skill when fundraising for the parish. Not to be outdone, Susan also learnt to free fall, and is one of the few women to have taken part in a 'four star' formation, jumping from twelve thousand feet. In due course Skye had seven puppies, and the Hughes kept the runt of the litter,

Septimus Spot. Then came Shuma: a champion ratter, despite having a steel-pinned leg after a five bar gate fall on her!

But it was with Harris, the most recent Jack Russell in the family, that Alan Hughes arrived in Berwick. The vicarage stands beside the seventeenth-century parish church of the Holy Trinity, in a square bordered by the Border Barracks, the first purpose-built barracks in England, and with walks available on the nearby fortified walls of the town. Harris's first walk was around the outside of the walls at night, and later that evening he disappeared, only to be found peering down a forty foot drop on the top of the ramparts. Local people soon became accustomed to the sight of Alan walking around with Harris draped round his shoulders, and children who attend the regular children's services are always enchanted by this habit. Harris is a true church dog, patrolling the churchyard, greeting visitors and parishioners alike, and even managing to join the welcome committee for a visit by Her Majesty the Queen.

The Rev. Philip Johnes and Annie

Holy Trinity Church, Llanegwadd

'I like dogs, because they regard you as equal, but a cat just looks down on you'

What could be more evocative of a certain quintessential Englishness, than the notion of an English vicar driving around his rural parish in a lovingly restored Morris Minor 1000, with his dog in the passenger seat? Philip Johnes is the epitome of this vision, and with a background in farm engineering systems, as well as having been a farmer himself, he is an ideal person to be vicar of Llanegwadd parish, in the upper reaches of the Towy Valley. This is working-dog country, and all three of Philip's dogs have had working dogs somewhere in their gene pool.

Philip's first dog was called Fred, a Scottish Terrier–Jack Russell cross who, as Philip discreetly put it, 'specialized in eyeing up lady dogs'. Fred used to accompany Philip to the local agricultural shows, where Philip stewarded dogs and pigs, and in view of Fred's proclivities for romance, he was securely tethered while Philip went about his show duties. But it never worked: somehow Fred always convinced some passing child that he was distressed, maltreated and needed freeing. Fred was then at liberty to do what he loved best – ensuring the continued puppy population of Llanegwadd.

Buster, another characterful dog with an excess of

libido, followed Fred. Ladies of the parish regularly turned up at the vicarage, arms full of puppies, demanding alimony. At which Philip decided that his next dog had better be female! So along came Annie, an anniversary gift from Philip's wife Gill. Annie is another cross, this time between a Jack Russell and a Border Collie. It must have

been a relief for her to come to the calm of Philip's home, as she had had to put up with some fairly disgraceful behaviour from her brother, a pugilist puppy, on the verge of being served with an Anti-Social Behaviour Order on account of his nipping the local police sergeant's dog. (Particularly irritating for the sergeant, who trains police dogs for the South Wales Police force.)

The Border Collie in Annie gazes longingly at the sheep in the surrounding fields, while the Jack Russell in her enjoys digging a good hole in the garden. As has been mentioned, she travels everywhere in the parish, sitting beside Philip in his Morris Minor, and when local dogs hear the car coming, they find a place to hide, as Annie has a fairly sharp way of dealing with other dogs. But with people, particularly children, Annie is lovely. When anyone approaches her she'll turn on her back, grunting with pleasure, as she waves her paws in the air. The neighbour's children have the best of both worlds with Annie – when she hears them in the garden, she leaps over the hedge to play, so they enjoy all the pleasure of a dog, without any of the hard work.

The Rev. Stella Langdon-Davies, Robbie and Flora

St Martin's Church and St Peter's Church, Old Herne

'Dogs are forgiving if you're short on time; they also give unconditional love'

These two bouncy, soccer-obsessed West Highland Terriers share their energetic lives with the Rev Stella Langdon-Davies and her husband. They live in Old Herne, where Stella is Vicar of St Martin's, a flint-towered medieval church, and St Peter's, a modern church in urban surroundings.

Prior to training for the priesthood, Stella had a career as a management consultant and taught at postgraduate level in counselling. The family has always had dogs in pairs, mostly Collies and Golden Retrievers; but since moving to Kent, from where they like to travel occasionally to France, they decided to go for West Highland Terriers, on the grounds that they are very domestic, have stamina, and need less exercise. In fact what they have found with Robbie and Flora, is that these two dogs effectively self-exercise. Most days the two dogs can be glimpsed hurtling around the garden, both attached firmly to opposite sides of a rapidly deflating football. The game is played according to two simple rules. The first is never to loosen your grip, the second is that a goal can only be scored by vigorously shaking both the ball and the other dog through the goal posts. Neither dog ever gives in, and eventually they collapse in utter exhaustion, still clamped to either side of the football. It's hard to believe that Robbie is eight years older than Flora.

Keeping a lower profile in the house, avoiding the soccer mania, are two cats, Tootsie and Sophie. The dogs and cats keep things on a friendly basis, especially as the cats have learned that the dogs won't chase them if they move slowly. So in the garden there are two rushing dogs, and, in the house, two slow-motion cats. Proving the détente between the species, Sophie the cat uses Flora as a mattress, sleeping draped over her – Flora views it more as having a feline blanket.

The dogs keep Stella company when she is working in her office, and love getting involved at the church. It's the strawberry teas in the summer that most catch their imagination, although they also take part in some of the services. Robbie wows the local primary school children in assemblies, while at Christmas, Flora pops out at the appropriate moment on a festive lead; this is all stage managed by Stella's husband Bob, who has to keep watch for Flo, the church cat, who is addicted to baptisms, weddings and all major services.

The Rev. Brian Lillington and Mollie

St Peter's, Yately

'I grew up with dogs. I love the companion-ship, watching a dog lie in front of the fire; being greeted by a wagging tail. It's the simple things about a dog that give pleasure'

Brian Lillington is one of a number of clerics featured in this book who made a move from the secular to the spiritual world later in life. Formerly Deputy Director of Social Services in Surrey, a visit to Iona in the 1980s set him on the path to becoming a non-stipendiary minister, at a point in life when many would settle for early retirement.

Mollie is the family Jack Russell, getting on in age, frail and not in very good health. Mollie has had her share of problems, including a broken ligament, loss of hearing, stomach problems (caused by the odd habit of eating gravel) and the onset of old age. But a Jack Russell never gives up, and even on a baking summer's day, she can sometimes be seen setting out unsteadily, heading in the direction of the nearby woodlands.

The Lillingtons originally fostered Mollie as a rescue dog; she came when Brian Lillington was away on Iona. She immediately took to Brian's wife Margaret, to the extent that when Brian came home, they had their work cut out to get Mollie to accept that he was part of the family too. Her age was never determined, although it is thought that she was some eight years old when she came. Jack Russells are not known for their love of cats, and the Lillingtons' cat Mindy was not particularly pleased about Mollie's arrival. But both animals were very British about the whole affair, maintaining a stiff and slightly wounded tolerance of each other – until it came to the question of food, when Mollie would shoulder Mindy aside and wolf down her share too.

Mollie's antics outside were typically Jack Russellish too. Walks on the nearby sandy heaths would conclude with Molly having to be dug out of a hole down which she had rushed in pursuit of a hapless rabbit. Her walks these days are more leisurely affairs, and on returning home, she gently clambers up a set of steps onto a settee, where she can take a nap, usually on top of the daily newspaper, which perforce remains unread until she has finished with it.

The Rev. Nicholas Lowton, and Asquith, Balfour and Canning

Cheltenham College, Cheltenham

'My dogs are my pastoral sidekicks. If I'm having a difficult conversation with a pupil, the dogs are invaluable'

Three Springer Spaniels live with the Rev. Nicholas Lowton, who is the Assistant Chaplain and a Housemaster at Cheltenham College. Named after leading British politicians (and with the same propensity to do exactly what they want) Asquith, Balfour and Canning are major features of life in the boarding house. These dogs have the best of both worlds: during term time they are the centre of attention with the boys, during holidays they go with Nicholas to his retreat in the Black Mountains in Herefordshire.

Nicholas had been very taken with the character of a Springer Spaniel owned by a colleague at Cheltenham, and in 1984 decided to get one for himself. Walpole, his first dog, spent a blissful thirteen years with Nicholas at the college; his ashes are scattered on the Black Hill made famous by the author Bruce Chatwin. Nicholas talks affectionately of Walpole as his 'pastoral sidekick'.

When Walpole was eight years old the vet advised Nicholas to get a Springer puppy to keep Walpole sprightly, and so Asquith came. This was an interesting event: Nicholas took a group of boys from the school with him to the breeder, and with the excitement of choosing Asquith, failed to notice that one of the boys had developed a slight bulge under his jacket – a bulge that wouldn't stop wriggling. On arrival at the college, the jacket burst open to reveal another happy, but unofficial, puppy, who was reluctantly returned to the breeder. Nonetheless the boarding house was buzzing with excitement at the official new arrival. Asquith adored Walpole, and Walpole was in general much taken with Asquith, except for the times Asquith hung off his ears. Nicholas has found that having the dogs around is an ideal antidote to home-sickness for his pupils.

Then Nicholas had a phone call to tell him that there was another puppy available, and Canning came to join the melange of spaniels and schoolboys, his arrival watched by the whole boarding house. The advantage of having puppies at Cheltenham is that there is no shortage of puppy sitters. And then came yet another phone call from the breeder, and as Nicholas recounts, 'I foolishly went along, just to see the litter!' The result was Balfour.

When term finishes, Nicholas and the dogs head for their retreat in the Black Mountains, and life takes on a new dimension: days of streaking over the mountains and splashing through streams.

The Rev. Tony Lynn and Borage

Church of St Peter and St Paul, Yattenden

'We have your dog here!'

The Rev. Tony Lynn was and still is a 'cat' person, but one who is undergoing the process of conversion to being a 'dog' person too. Assisting him on this sometimes frustrating journey is a shiny, lively young black Labrador called Borage.

Tony Lynn was happily settled as Team Minister in the sleepy Home Counties village of Yattendon. His cats, Chorlton cum Hardy, wandered in and out of the rectory, went off on their country walks, and kept him company in the evenings; and then one of Tony's parishioners, who had a black Labrador called Basil (after the herb, not the proprietor of Fawlty Towers), introduced him to a puppy called Dill. Dill was one of a litter of black Labrador pups that had resulted from Basil's regular trips to the 'Love Shack' breeding centre. By his own admission Tony fell in love with black Labradors at first sight of this little puppy, and after some reflection, decided to go and have a look at the rest of the litter. Out of the herbally-named puppies, he picked out one particular fellow who seemed to show particular spirit and charm – Borage.

Borage and Tony went home, and life changed forever. Following instructions to ignore any crying, Tony bedded the new puppy down in the kitchen, and went to bed, bracing himself for a night of howling and crying from the kitchen. What actually happened was that he didn't sleep a wink, while Borage slept like a log. The cats, though, were horrified at the change wrought in their lives. What was

wander, not because he's unhappy at home, but because he just loves everyone so much, and wants to say hello.

Tony's aim is to get Borage settled enough to be able to go to services, and to come with him to the two local schools. Borage has pre-empted the school visits, mind you, nipping off and hopping the fence into the school playground adjacent to the rectory. This is one absence where Tony doesn't have to wait for the 'We have your dog here' phone call: the squeals of delight from the playground are a sure sign that Borage is at the centre of attention of a group of children, who are only too delighted to have him come and distract them from the formal obligations of the school day.

their owner doing, bringing in this bouncy black dog who wanted to play with them non-stop? The cats responded by changing their routines, choosing routes inaccessible to Borage - but more often than not ending up cornered under a chair, with Borage huffing and snuffling, pleading with them to come out. The situation didn't improve much as he got older (and larger) - he still can't understand why Chorlton cum Hardy avoid him.

Over time, Borage was introduced to the parish, One particular parishioner started to carry a bag of sweets to offer Borage when they met, and now that he has found out where she lives, he regularly goes AWOL, ending up standing up at her kitchen window, waiting anxiously to see whether he will get additional rations. He does tend to

The Rev. Philip Marsh, Frisbee and Muppet

St John's Church, Werrington

'Having animals in the family is, for us, just a natural thing'

This is a large busy family: Philip Marsh and his wife Mandy have four children, Joshua, Charlie, Blain and Scarlet, and their ages range from nine years down to five months. In addition, there is a black cat called Stout, an amiable mutt called Muppet, and a canine compilation called Frisbee. Muppet is clearly a standard pick 'n' mix mongrel (with a bit of collie thrown in), and a friendly fellow he is too. Frisbee is ostensibly a cross between a Gordon Setter and a lurcher, although one could be forgiven for thinking she is a miniature Irish Wolfhound.

The first animal to greet one at the vicarage is usually Stout, a burly and slightly battle-scarred veteran black cat hanging around the front garden. Her message is, 'It's good to see a new face around, but if I were you, I'd stay outside. It's quieter, and you won't have to contend with the dogs.' And as the front door is opened, Stout walks off, as if to say 'OK. Don't listen, but I did warn you.'

Philip, a former science teacher, describes Frisbee as 'a quantum dog, who occupies more space than she constitutes'. It's easy to see why: with her mad energy she appears to be in several places at once. Almost as Frisbee bundles through the door, she reappears at one's shoulder, grinning inanely. It's quite charming, if a little unnerving.

As a puppy she was all legs, and is not, so Phil says, very bright. Her carousing round the house usually results in her barging into people without realising. Blain, the Marshes' three year old son, regularly gets tipped over as Frisbee passes. Frisbee is fascinated by Stout, with whom he's very affectionate, always wanting to play. But Stout is not fascinated by Frisbee, having had to learn early on to evade Frisbee's attempts at friendliness (which consist of trying to hold Stout down so that he can give him a good licking). He tolerates her, but usually retreats to a vantage point on the stairs from where he looks on stoically as Frisbee cannons her way round the house.

Muppet, on the other hand, is used to cats: Stout was a childhood companion of hers, although the truth is that the relationship was not close – more a 'live and let live' arrangement. According to Philip, Muppet is much brighter than Frisbee. She does evince this common canine problem, though: show her a ball, and all vestige of restraint and intelligence disappears, only re-emerging after any balls have been safely hidden away.

The Rev. Canon Roland Meredith and Smudge

Christ Church Cathedral, Oxford

'I've always had dogs, and collies are my favourites'

The Meredith family divides into two distinct camps so far as domestic pets are concerned. On the one hand, Susan Meredith, who stewards at Christ Church Cathedral, and works in the bookshop, is a cat person. Canon Roland Meredith, on the other hand, is most definitely a dog person. The fourth generation of his family to be a clergyman, Roland Meredith has had forty-three years of dogs – four of which have been Border Collies, his favourite breed. Smudge is the fourth collie, and lives with the Merediths in their Eynsham home.

The other four-footed occupant of the family home is Pussy, a rescue cat, and Smudge has yet to learn that he can't always successfully boss the cat around; he persists in constant attempts to round up and corral Pussy, which usually end up with Smudge going rapidly into reverse gear as Pussy decides that enough is enough, and advances on him, hissing and bristling – an altogether alarming sight for a lively but nervous Border Collie.

Smudge's nervousness arises from his puppy period, when he lived with an elderly couple and was unable to get out and about. At a year old, Smudge went to a rescue centre; luckily Roland Meredith was looking for a Border Collie, and after only four days in the rescue centre, Smudge went to his new family. Although he's still a bit highly strung, he's getting precisely what he really needed as a puppy – exercise, and lots of it. He does a regular round of Christ Church Meadows, through which – to his delight – flows the River Isis. He is a passionate swimmer, a skill he tries to combine with his instincts to herd: Smudge can often be seen, paddling frantically, trying to direct quacking ducks to the bank. His interest in rounding up swans and punts is discouraged as much as possible, however. As well as accompanying Roland Meredith when he goes to Christ Church Cathedral, Smudge also gets regular visits to the open spaces of nearby Blenheim Palace, as well as two woods local to home in which he is free to roam. So his lack of exercise as a young puppy may one day be adequately compensated for, thanks to his new life with Roland.

The Rev. Dr Vaughan Roberts and Ella

Collegiate Church of St Mary, Warwick

'I enjoy the company of a dog; and having one means that I take exercise too. It's a symbiotic relationship'

When the Roberts' son John's voice broke, he had to leave the choir at Wells Cathedral; and, as is customary, he received a sum of accrued royalties and fees as his share from the proceeds of the choir's commercial activities. He had wanted to buy a puppy for some time, and now had some bargaining power. Firm rules were laid down: if John was to have a dog, he'd have to walk her, feed her and train her. John wanted a gun-dog, and eventually found a breeder in Herefordshire who agreed to let a puppy go to the Roberts household for a few weeks' trial. Predictably, Ella – as the puppy was named – never went back.

Although Ella was nominally John's dog, his parents and sister had topped up the purchase price, so Ella instantly became a family dog. John set about arranging for Ella to be trained, with the help of a local gamekeeper: he wanted Ella to realise her retriever instincts. The training concluded successfully after several weeks, and Ella went on her first shoot. During the hustle and bustle of preparation, Ella stood attentively, looking every bit the classic gun-dog; but as the first shot was fired, she turned tail, and disappeared at high speed under the nearest Land Rover. John had apparently found himself a pacifist gun dog! (The only things she ever retrieves are some rather soggy and well-chewed inanimate stuffed objects that might at one time have been dog toys!)

From Somerset, the Roberts family moved to Warwick, where Vaughan Roberts had been appointed Team Rector of Warwick, and Vicar of St Mary's. John and his sister Becky went off to university, their mother Mandy was occupied with teaching, and Ella became Vaughan Roberts's personal companion by default. She's a great dog for a town vicarage, delivering a fusillade of barks at the sound of the doorbell, but with the family she's as soft as butter. Ella has played a starring role in pet services, and has carved out a role as clearer-up at the parish barbeques (sometimes clearing up a little more than is welcome).

She has some excellent walks nearby that include the canal and the River Avon. She's forever dragging out pieces of wood that are twice her size, and is always delighted to see the swans. She splashes over to them enthusiastically, and then splashes away with equal energy, as the swans make their disapproval known.

The Rev. Claire Robson, and Max and Alice

St Paul's Cathedral, City of London

*'Max and Alice make me laugh, although
I suspect that they may be laughing at me'*

Claire Robson, a Minor Canon at St Paul's Cathedral, is a familiar figure around the cathedral precincts: her height contrasts with the diminutive stature of the two miniature long-haired dachshunds who regularly accompany her. I have always been a larger dog type of person, I must confess, but Max and Alice confound every prejudice that I have had about small dogs. They are, to put it simply, hilariously crazy. There's about three years age difference between them, but they both spend all their time playing. It's that ball thing. Claire's house rumbles with balls rolling from one side of the room to the other, accompanied by the frantic scrabbling of two sets of paws trying to get first possession of it.

Max is, on first impression, the slightly sharper of the two, and when he drops a ball, squeaky toy, or whatever at one's feet (which is to say, at every second moment), he has a disconcerting way of looking at you rather than the object, and appears to be saying something along the lines of 'I'm sure that even you can't be so stupid as to not know what I require of you!' Alice, being a little more tactful, sits to the side while this goes on, ready to dash in and seize the ball while Max is distracted by the task of psychological persuasion of the human - so perhaps Max isn't so bright after all.

Part of Claire's pastoral remit is the Choir School, where Max and Alice are superstars. Max is *ex officio* bedtime monitor for the choristers, a job he embraces perhaps over-enthusiastically, as he would like his duties to consist mainly of leaping onto every bed. As lights-out approaches, Max will frantically hunt for a ball to distract everyone with. But he and Alice also fill a more demanding role, that of banishing the odd tear of home-sickness. And it is remarkable to see how quickly both dogs can turn a tear into a laugh.

Both dogs delight in living in a Close where there are families with young children, though I wonder how much the Dean appreciates the excited barking outside his window when Alice, Max and the neighbouring children really swing into action. Where both dogs really score domestically, though, is as house watchdogs. Max in particular is capable of a truly macho bark. If a stranger approaches, he will know to beware! That is, until Max ruins the whole effect by revealing himself at the window and betraying his small size.

The Rev. Craig Smith and Jack

Christchurch, Catshill, Holy Trinity Church and St Mary's, Dodford

'Jack is my champion stress reliever'

Jack is a purebred Border Collie, who lives with Craig Smith and his family at their vicarage in the (perhaps inappropriately named) Worcestershire village of Catshill. Jack's activities as a puppy, when he came to the family home, then in Essex, have had an impact on domestic arrangements ever since. As a young dog, Jack couldn't resist chewing telephone cables: Craig recalls wryly that, being in the early days of his curacy, not being able to receive phone calls was not such a bad idea. Jack also ate bits of furniture – creating his own version of 'dogtooth' decoration – and in the interest of having tables with four rather than three legs, Craig's wife Sheila took charge. So the vicarage at Catshill is arranged with the living room, kitchen and study upstairs, and bedrooms and bathrooms downstairs. The living quarters in the upstairs of the house are entirely out of bounds, except for one small room with a gate, where Jack will wait cheerfully for any sign of an outing. He doesn't normally have to wait very long, as he always accompanies Craig when he takes a prayer walk around the parish, or when he's on local rounds.

Jack is a very playful dog. He's often seen dashing around the churchyard in pursuit of his favourite toy, bounding energetically over tombstones and dodging round memorials. The churchyard has its fair share of rather mournful Victorian monuments and Jack's joyful antics rather brighten the place up. Craig places a high value on Jack's unfailingly cheerful nature. It does him good to go out with Jack, especially after a difficult parish council meeting: 'Jack just takes my mind away from the preoccupations of everyday life.'

Craig believes strongly in taking his ministry to the community, and does so in part through an ingenious event called Pints of View, at which one can talk with Craig over a pint of 'Do I need 100% proof', 'Taste and see Premium Spirit', or 'Very very bitter (God is Dead)' beer, a series of encounters with members of the local community at the local pub. Jack has responded well to the idea of these sessions, particularly if there would be a dish of locally brewed beer at the end for him – but so far, Craig has been immune to Jack's pleading!

The Rev. Dr Alan Sowerbutts and Albert

**Church of St John the Evangelist,
Read-in-Whalley**

*'Albert encourages me to take walks on
the moors, and to remind me what it is
like to play'*

Alan Sowerbutts and his wife Gillian live in the mill village of Read, on the edge of the Lancashire moors. A Lancashire man born and bred, Alan has worked in parishes throughout Lancashire. The family's first dog was a Cairn Terrier named Mandy, whose role was intended to be providing company for Gillian Sowerbutts, since Alan was out for so much of the time. It was an odd, if fortuitous choice, as Gillian had been most definitely a cat person: the family menagerie at Read comprised five cats and two geese. Hardly the most welcome environment for a dog. But Mandy's presence turned out to be highly beneficial for the incumbent cats. Mandy had to learn to run fast to get away from these notoriously bad-tempered birds, although she eventually got her own back, as evinced by a scattering of goose tail feathers, and the two geese who suddenly ran away, honking in alarm, whenever Mandy appeared in the garden.

Mandy's reception from the cats was different. They were an argumentative bunch, always squabbling amongst themselves, and much too busy arguing over their own hierarchy to take much notice of Mandy. The dog became something of a peacemaker, and in doing so, inadvertently established herself as the 'boss'.

So dogs became a fixture in the Sowerbutts family, with the household menagerie further supplemented by the arrival of a Border Collie cross called Chloe, who came following Mandy's death at 13 years, from the austerely named Bleak Halt Animal Rescue Centre. She died of a serious illness after only three months, and Albert came as her replacement. Albert – with such a perfectly no-nonsense Lancashire name – also had some Border Collie in him. He was a bit subdued when he first came, and even now in the house Albert is quiet; he loves to snooze, is devoted to Gillian, and generally ignores all visitors (once he has barked at their arrival!)

But when he had settled in, Albert did develop some unusual characteristics. The principal of these was, and still is, retrieving a ball. There is nothing particularly unusual in a dog fetching: what sets Albert apart is his apparent belief that the ball itself is alive. So sometimes, instead of returning it to the thrower, he'll drop the ball and stare at it in tense anticipation, expecting it to move of its own volition. Albert in the garden is as likely to be seen glued to the spot, watching a ball that, barring divine intervention, is clearly going nowhere. At other times Albert, having been chasing the ball, will stay stock still, muscles tensed for a spring, looking at a place on the ground where he is convinced that the ball ought to be. So the mad dashing ball-chaser becomes an apparently purposeless statue-like figure, staring at a patch of grass where a ball might have been, or should be.

Winding their sinuous way through all this running and standing still are Nelson and Fido, the sole survivors of the original group of five cats. Nelson likes Albert, and often butts up to him in a companionable way. But Albert doesn't reciprocate: his only concern is to find the ball. Nelson clearly sympathises, and I suspect that he's hinting to Albert that it may be time for him to come inside, take a calming draught, and tell him all about it.

Father Mark Stafford and Nina

St Michael the Archangel, Retford

'The best thing about talking to Nina is that she doesn't have an opinion'

In a family with three daughters, Fr Mark, a former engineer and specialist in transport research, ensures that, as the sole male, he guards his territory carefully. 'With an all-female household, you need beer and cars, otherwise you end up plaiting your hair.' The Stafford household is a combination of femininity, restored vintage cars and motorcycles, and a female long-haired Alsatian called Nina. Fr Mark had experience of both dogs and transport from his youth. His father had a fondness for Jack Russells, which he used to take to and from work with him in his jacket pocket. But it wasn't until he was appointed to an urban parish in Stafford that he and his wife Tracey decided that they needed a dog of their own. Living in a tough neighbourhood, the family had several unpleasant encounters, and on one occasion Fr Mark had been attacked.

One day, they happened to spot an Alsatian breeder's house. They decided to call in, and were introduced to a long-haired Alsatian puppy, and before long they found themselves taking her home.

Nina, as she was named, had one of the most cosseted puppyhoods imaginable. With the Stafford's three daughters, Abby, Carla and Beth, in attendance, Nina's every want was attended to. Father Mark drew the line when Nina started to appear with plaits. 'I'm afraid', he admonished, 'that any miscreant confronted by an Alsatian with plaits in her hair is likely to die laughing.'

Nina's hair was duly unplaited, and she grew into a trustworthy, affectionate and very protective dog. Her first test was when an adjacent garage was taken over by a group of drug dealers, who started to harass the Staffords. After coming face to face with Nina, straining at the end of her leash in a most unclerical and menacing manner, they decided to shut up shop there and then. But Nina also made many friends: people who would not normally even think of stopping to talk to a vicar, would happily stop and admire Nina.

In his present parish, where things are somewhat less threatening, Fr Mark and Nina are a familiar sight, tootling through town in a gleaming open-topped Austin Seven, with Fr Mark in front, gingerly crunching his way through the gears, and Nina in the back, gazing regally out at the passers-by who stop to watch this wonderfully English combination of vicar, vintage car and dog.

Father Terry Steele and Jack

Church of St Peter and St Paul, Burgh-le-Marsh

'Jack is my friend and companion – and he's the right size!'

Lincolnshire born and bred Fr Terry Steele, Rural Dean of Calcewaithe and Candleshow, is a latecomer to the joys of owning a dog. Much of his working life had been spent in retail, and he was eventually made redundant. He was already thinking about ordination, and at a meeting with a vicar in his hometown of Grantham he had been very taken with the vicar's beagle. So one morning, he left a note for his mother that simply said 'Gone to get a dog.' He went with a beagle because it was the right size for him, and would, so he was informed, be good with children. So along came Sam, who duly accompanied him through his ordination, and his early days as vicar of four Lincolnshire parishes.

Sam was a regular churchgoer, happy to curl up in any warm corner, as long as he could hear Father Terry's voice. In children's services he'd howl along with the recorders, although whether from anguish or a wish to join in is not clear, and was a regular invitee to weddings and baptisms. Sam died on All Souls Day 1997, and by pure chance, one week later Father Terry found Jack.

Jack is another beagle, a true test of Father Terry's patience and tolerance, who as a puppy was known as Jack the Ripper. He'd chew anything: diaries, carpets, shoes, slippers, but despite Fr Terry's vicarage soon looking like the aftermath of a giant moth attack, man and dog rapidly developed a close and affectionate bond. He goes to church with Father Terry, where his habit of snoring loudly is picked up by Father Terry's microphone. It is a very consolatory Jack who often attends funerals.

He also goes to all four local schools for assemblies, where some mistake his curious habit of lowering his head to his owner for a ritual bow. Jack is perfect with young children, who generally look after Jack during these assemblies, and while one might question how much they are actually taking in from the formal assembly, they are certainly learning how to take joy in one part of God's creation. At the end of each term there is usually a gift of a bag of sweets for Jack, although in truth he has more than his fair share of sugary goodies. One of Father Terry's parishioners works at a chocolate factory, and is forever bringing round bags of sample confections, which are hastily put away in a kitchen drawer. But Jack knows which one; that beagle nose could track down the delicious smell of chocolate from a mile away.

To get at the contents of this drawer, Jack performs the most melodramatic pantomime. He sits on his hindquarters, forepaws raised and folded over his chest, only moving his eyes, to see if anyone is taking any notice. If this doesn't work, he sits looking anxiously at the drawer, then repeats the sitting-up business from the other side. It is a great comic routine, but never works, as human chocolate is not good for dogs. So it is that Jack retains a sprightliness as he walks up the path to the church with Father Terry, to fall fast asleep under his stall once more.

The Rev. Juliet Stephenson, and Hector the Rector

St Swithun's Church, Retford

'My days off walking around Clumber Park Lake with Hector are a joyous way of being with the creator and the created.'

The Rev. Juliet Stephenson had promised her family that, once they were out of the cramped college house where they had been living while she completed her theological studies, they'd get a dog. And in fulfilling this promise she took no half measures, acquiring a Weimaraner. The cute rabbit-sized puppy grew rapidly to fill the folds of skin that had virtually hidden his features, and suddenly there was Hector, boar-hunter by breeding, and 'Rector' by default!

As a puppy, Hector won the hearts of a tight-knit group of three parishioners, Doris, Winnie and Rosemary (with a collective age of two hundred), who cradled him in a blanket, and have become his adopted 'aunties' – although trying to cradle Hector in a blanket these days would require a crane! Right from the start it was clear that Hector was going to be a church dog, and he'd go with Juliet when she went to practice for mass, standing up when the vicar stood, walking to the altar when she did, and standing with his paws on the altar. 'All he needed,' says Juliet, 'was a dog collar of the clerical variety.'

One of the problems of being a large dog who really isn't aware of his size, is that Hector actually thinks that he makes a perfectly acceptable lap dog, and once the Stevensons' children are in bed, insists on trying to climb onto Juliet's lap, or that of her husband, Phill. Hector has some other odd habits too: if Juliet stops to talk to parishioners in the street, Hector positions his considerable weight on her feet, clearly more interested in being on his way than in passing the time of day chatting. Nor does he care for people reading newspapers instead of spending time with him. Phill Stevenson's Saturday morning reading is regularly interrupted by Hector as he shoves the paper aside. However, his oddest custom is his early morning cup of tea; and not just any old tea, either: Earl Grey is his preference, and it's served to him out of a special mug.

One of his favourite haunts is nearby Clumber Park, where Hector learned how to swim the hard way, by falling in the lake. And this is where his birthday is celebrated: the ice cream vendor has created a special cut-price dog ice cream, and Hector is one of his best customers.

The Rev. Phillip Storr Venter and Haik

All Saints' Church, Highgate

'I've had dogs since childhood, and hate the feeling of being without one'

It was this sense of lacking a dog that inspired Phillip Storr Venter to acquire a Caucasian Shepherd puppy from a shepherd on the slopes of Mount Ara (which overlooks Mount Ararat). He had accepted a seven year posting to Armenia in a joint rôle as attaché for Regional Development at the British Embassy, and the Archbishop of Canterbury's representative to the Armenian and Georgian Orthodox Churches. With a background in international insurance law, and third world and emerging country economics, Phillip has travelled extensively on behalf of the British government and other international organisations, combining these duties with being Priest in Charge of All Saint's, in Highgate, North London.

The well-travelled Haik is obviously devoted to Phillip. He's a friendly dog, but it is quite clear where his principal duty lies – in guarding his owner. Haik is a magnificent example of an ancient breed of sheep-guarding, rather than sheep-herding, dogs. Traditionally, the breed has the outer part of its ears docked at birth, in order to make it more difficult for the traditional enemy, the wolf, to grab during a fight.

When Phillip's time in Armenia came to a close, he and Haik set out on the long overland journey back to England in a red-plated diplomatic vehicle; food was bought at the roadside on the way. Haik sat quietly, watching as the world passed by. Even quarantine in England didn't bother him. Frequent visits by Philip kept him cheerful, and Haik took the transition from his native Armenian mountains to urban London without blinking, although he still has a passion for the wild: he loves to roam the water meadows of the River Lea, one of his favourite walks. And at home he disdains the comfort of a soft bed, preferring to sleep on a hard floor; perhaps there's a deep-buried memory of the Armenian mountainsides where his ancestors roamed.

The Rev. Patrick Taylor and Bertie

St Alphege Church, Solihull

'A dog makes a place feel like home'

Patrick Taylor and his wife Laura were looking for an excuse to get a dog. They had moved into a large house with a park behind, through which Patrick walked each day to and from the Parish Church of St Alphege. Not having had pets before, they'd had a look at some Labradors, and decided that they were all 'barking mad'. (Now Labrador owners, and I've been one myself, all know that they are lovely dogs, but you have to admit that they can be a bit, well, flakey.) Then they visited a local Dogs Trust rescue centre, but they had no luck finding a suitable dog – until, as they left after a third unsuccessful visit, Laura spotted a greyhound, watching them closely, his nose pressed against the glass. They arranged another 'meet and greet' and the deal was done: Bertie was 'tall, dark, and handsome'; a retired racing greyhound (and a regular race winner in his time) who leant winsomely against Patrick's legs, looking up as if to say 'Well, you haven't had an animal before, and I haven't had a home before, not as such, so how about it?'

So after a home inspection and a pre-adoption talk, an apprehensive Patrick and Laura went to collect Bertie. At first Bertie just stood, politely, as if he didn't want to push his luck. Like all racing greyhounds, he had never known what it was to play – so Patrick and Laura had to encourage him into a second late puppyhood, learning to relax, to enjoy playing and just hanging out.

In return for the gift of family life, Bertie has become an ace companion: he walks through the park with Laura when she goes to meet Patrick from evening prayers, and does first-class 'ice-breaking' when he's out with Patrick ('Look Mummy, it's a horse!'). Bertie is the first to greet visitors to the house, and both Patrick and Laura say that one can't overestimate the value of a dog at home, especially after a hard or stressful day.

The Rev. Canon Tim Thompson and Penny

St Peter's Church, Gowts and
St Botolph's, Lincoln

'Dogs and vicars are like strawberries and cream'

Canon Tim Thompson's first dog, a West Highland Terrier called Tosh, nearly ruined his prospects of getting married. During a first meeting between prospective parents-in-law, which took place in a car park at Polperro – an odd place for such an encounter, it sounds more reminiscent of a showdown than a joyful celebration of an engagement – Tosh bit Tim Thompson's future wife Babs on the wrist. So the question of dogs must have been a delicate subject in the family for some while, and certainly dogs are not named again in the family history until the talk turns to the Thompsons' first vicarage dog, a black farm-bred Labrador called Sam.

When they first met Sam, the brother of a champion gundog, the Thompsons thought him a bit lively, but were assured by a good friend, who was a leading light in the tertiary Franciscans, that he would calm down. Given their earlier experience with Tosh, and the fact that Franciscans are always optimists, this should surely have been a red light but no, Sam came to the parish in Grimsby where Tim was curate. A dear old lady, bearing a bottle of homemade sloe gin, was there to welcome Tim home. Sam decided to join in the fun too, standing with his paws on the old lady's shoulders and pinning her to the wall while he gave her an enthusiastic licking. After Sam had been pried off, Tim saw the old lady home, wondering perhaps if she didn't need the bottle of sloe gin rather more than he. Sam truly had a knack for creating inadvertent havoc in family life, and overexcitement on the children's birthdays in particular led to his running away from threats of being neutered. The family would then have to scour the area looking for him.

Tim was impressed by Sam's apparent sixth sense: one evening they walked over to the vestry where a body was awaiting burial, set for the following day. Sam point blank refused to go in. The following day, the day of the funeral, he came over again, and Tim discovered that, rather than having an incredible sixth sense, Sam actually had an aversion to parquet wood flooring, and couldn't have given a hoot as to whether there were one or ten corpses awaiting burial.

Penny, their current dog, was a fiftieth birthday present from Tim's wife: he had been given the choice of a Labrador or a car, and decided that he'd be better off quietly buying himself a car a bit later, and went for the dog option. Penny was a sweet dog, the best behaved of all their dogs to date, with the disarming, if slightly uncomfortable, habit of sitting on one's feet. She attends all Tom's weddings and funerals and evinces none of Sam's melodramatic antics. She could almost have been a show dog, except for a nick in one ear, but has managed still to produce two Crufts-winning puppies. Penny is a good barker, too, although Tim is concerned that, if she was let out from behind the closed door, the barking would stop immediately and she would actually be more likely to lick any unwanted visitor off the premises than anything.

Father Richard Warhurst and Wystan

Church of St Nicolas, Old Shoreham

'Dogs are expressive, affectionate and loyal. They sense your distress, and they never repeat what they're told!'

Fr Richard is the assistant priest at St Nicolas, Old Shoreham and St Mary de Haura, New Shoreham, and dogs have been a part of his life since he was eight years old. Two border collies grew up with him, and it was only when he went to university that life became dogless.

A few years ago Fr Richard decided that the time had come to get another dog, only there was a snag: his wife to be, Joanne, had never had pets, and was less convinced that a dog was a good idea. Fr Richard, never daunted, pointed out all of the advantages, benefits and joys of dog ownership, and through a subtle process of attrition managed to establish that the acquisition of a dog would be the principal feature of an informal pre-nuptial agreement – and Joanne, without quite knowing how, found herself giving her future husband a wedding gift in the form of an English Springer Spaniel, Wystan.

Wystan's pedigree name – Izumis, son of Preacher Man – seemed to Joanne an auspicious sign, and home he came. From the moment he arrived, Wystan was obviously intent on testing Joanne to the limit, almost as if he knew of her lack of experience of living with a dog. How could she have known that she was bringing into her life a turbo-charged, irrepressible and unstoppable creature, whose chief aim seemed to be to do everything that he was not supposed to do? His first meeting with mother-in-law was far from a success, and it was only after a real battle of wills that Wystan even started to acquire the essential characteristics of a clerical dog – dignified, soulful and empathetic.

There is clearly some way to go, however. From being a puppy that would flinch at the sight of a puddle, Wystan has since become a sort of canine estuary hovercraft (albeit a malfunctioning one – swimming, rather than hovering). His soul is in the walks and the great outdoors, specifically the tidal reaches of the River Adur at low tide, in acres of glorious mud. And he has an obsession with making friends with swans: Wystan has got it into his head that the swans on the river actually want him to play with the cygnets. This is a barmy, loveable dog.

So when Fr Richard talks about Wystan 'never repeating anything he's told', it's clearly more a question of Wystan being incapable of remembering anything he's been told for more than five seconds.

The Rev. Tony Whipp, Muffin and Charles

Church of St Ebba, Ebchester

'My dogs get me out and exercising. They are great company when I'm by myself at home, and have a homely effect on nervous or distressed visitors. My dogs open doors and ease inhibitions'

When Tony Whipp wants to be alone with his thoughts, he heads for the River Derwent, which flows through the valley beneath Ebchester, where he and his wife Shelagh live. With him on his walks go their two dogs, Charles, a bouncy Springer Spaniel, and Muffin, a Border Terrier with, it seems, a built-in perpetual-motion engine. Charles always dives straight into the river, dragging endless pieces of driftwood to the banks, while Muffin simply runs round Tony in endless circles, desperately hoping that a treat will drop out of his pocket.

Tony Whipp is a former soldier and now Rector of three parishes, Ebchester, Medomsly and Hamsterly. He and his wife have had a long succession of pets, some of whom arrived in fairly dramatic fashion. In his former parish of Hartlepool, Tony Whipp was just starting the annual harvest festival when a cat staggered into the church, in a highly distressed state. The service paused while Tony and his congregation went to the latecomer's aid. The congregation voted unanimously that the cat should, if possible, live at the vicarage.

Muffin, meanwhile, was found in a box at the side of the road, and adopted by Tina, the Whipps' daughter. She brought Muffin home to be nursed by the family's doughty German Shepherd, Gypsy, and the two dogs became inseparable. Ever an explorer, Muffin is always disappearing on some mysterious errand or the other, but when Gypsy became incurably ill, the caring roles were reversed: Muffin was keen to help with the nursing, and was inconsolable when Gypsy died. She wouldn't eat, and lost interest in all her normal activities – but then came Charles. Muffin immediately perked up, and fussed around Charles, showing him where the bed was, where to eat, and generally showered him with motherly love.

Father Richard Williams and Jimmy

St Mary's Church, Hay-on-Wye

'It takes a dog to make us fully human: a dog knows he is deeply loved – unlike many humans.'

Jimmy is Fr Richard's third dog, succeeding Murphy, who had been with Fr Richard since his ordination, and Jaffa, a loveable orange canine eccentricity, with the head of a Labrador and the body of a Corgi, who is now buried in the vicarage garden. After a period without a dog, a parishioner suggested that a Standard Poodle would be a perfect companion for Fr Richard. He visited a breeder, where Jimmy effectively chose him. Fr Richard describes how, 'As I left after my first visit, Jimmy gazed sadly after me through the gates, and when I went back, Jimmy just went wild with excitement.'

So Jimmy came back to the parish of St Mary's, in Hay-on-Wye, that Fr Richard has so much affection for. 'It has the easiness of border country, and the parishioners make it easy to love them', he comments. It is a perfect setting for Fr Richard, a man of the arts – an accomplished organist, pianist and poet – in a town celebrated for its literary associations. Jimmy shares Fr Richard's love of music, often lying at his master's feet while he plays the piano at home. Jimmy's musical appreciation extends further than the house, too: he often attends local concerts, where he sits motionless until the final note has died away

and then, as the applause breaks out, Jimmy gets carried away. Thinking that the applause is for him, he dashes to the front, and turns to face the audience, tail wagging in acceptance of the accolades. Most visiting conductors view this with amusement, although occasionally the smiles can seem a bit forced.

Jimmy has become a well-known figure in Hay-on-Wye, a town with more than its share of eccentric characters, and now bears the title 'St James, Knight of the Black Mountains', conferred on him by the self-styled ruler of Hay-on-Wye, Richard Booth. He regularly rubs shoulders with many of the famous Literature Festival worthies, as well as being a frequent browser in the bookshops.

Parish life is very much Jimmy's thing, and he's a well-loved feature of St Mary's. Whether it's helping to pull the Angelus bell, escorting a bride down the aisle or just sitting quietly through mass or compline, Jimmy is always there.

The Rev. Nick Woodcock and Bertie

Church of St Peter and St Paul, Lavenham

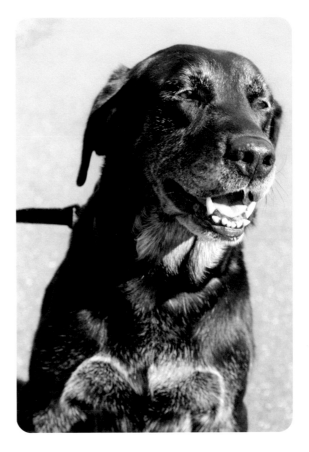

'Bertie is a naval dog really, without the slightest interest in smartening himself up for parade'

The answer phone message at Lavenham Rectory, where the Rev. Nick Woodcock, Rector of Lavenham, lives with his wife Christine, is not as decorous as it was intended to be. It all came about from a trick taught to Bertie, their burly, black Labrador, by the Woodcocks' sons. The theory was that any burglar coming across Bertie would tell him to be quiet. Therefore, if he was trained to bark at the command 'Be Quiet', any potential mischief-doer would be confounded. But the whole thing backfired. Getting a black Labrador to do anything on command, except eating, is quite hard. They are strong on valour, but not quite so much in the brain department, and by the time it was realised that Bertie would also need to be taught to be quiet on the opposite command 'Start Barking', it was already too late. Bertie's powers of concentration had been exhausted. As a result, the message on the Rectory answer phone consists simply of Nick Woodcock blurting out, 'This is Lavenham Rectory. You know what to do' – the rest is drowned out in an uproar of Bertie's barking. Bertie, ever-present at Nick's side, was repeatedly told to be quiet while Nick recorded his answer phone greeting; but after many attempts, Nick simply gave up.

Bertie first reported for duty at Portsmouth, where Nick was a sea-going naval chaplain. It is a tradition that naval personnel have black dogs – which ruled out Jack Russells, hitherto the favourite breed of the Woodcocks. Bertie became very friendly with the family's black cat, Billy, with whom he'd go on long walks round the base. He is a valiant dog, as the marks on his ears bear out. One day he was walking around the Dartmouth Naval base with Christine when a pair of unsupervised attack dogs spotted Christine, and went for her. Bertie sprang to her defence,

managing to keep the attack dogs at bay until their handler came, and to this day bears their teeth marks on his ears – nature's medal of valour. But other than this, Bertie is basically laid back; too laid back for his own good in some ways. When Nick Woodcock was precentor at Ely Cathedral, he'd just sit there woofing while a pushy rat would stroll in every night to empty Bertie's food dish, carrying it nonchalantly into his pantry behind a bookcase. The rat wasn't bothered one bit by Bertie's barking. And it took a good dose of rat deterrent to persuade him to move out.

At home in Lavenham, the only animals he has to deal with are Jimmy Hendrix, a black cat of indeterminate origin who belongs to the Woodcocks' younger son Edward, and marauding Muntjac deer, who invade the garden and eat all the flowers. What he really likes to do is to doze at Nicks feet, grunting and snorting with sleepy pleasure every now and then, or to sit and chat with visitors in the churchyard. He sometimes sits in the church and chats with visitors too, although one gets the impression that his mind is not really on the job, by the way his eyes keep flicking longingly towards the homemade cake stall manned by the ladies of the parish.